©Copyright 2005
Centering Corporation
All Rights Reserved.

www.centering.org

Additional copies may be ordered from:

Centering Corporation
PO Box 4600
Omaha, NE 68104

Phone: 402-553-1200
Fax: 402-553-0507

Plans

Using story books to help elementary school age children understand death and the grieving process

WRITTEN BY: GERALDINE HAGGARD
DESIGNED BY: KNOLL GILBERT

This book is dedicated to the families who come to Journey of Hope and the facilitators who work in the program.

The program provides support for grieving families and is made possible by many wonderful people who spend many volunteer hours planning and working in the program.

Library of Congress Cataloging-in-Publication Data

Haggard, Geraldine, 1929-
  Plans : using story books to help explain death and the grieving process to elementary school age children : a Centering Corporation resource / by Geraldine Haggard.
    p.cm.
ISBN 1-56123-187-8 (alk. paper)
  1. Children and death--Study and teaching. 2. Bereavement in children--Study and teaching. 3. Thanatology. 4. Death in literature--Study and teaching. 5. Bereavement in literature--Study and teaching. 6. Storytelling. I. Centering Corporation. II. Title.

BF723.D3H34 2005
155.9'37'0834--dc22

2005049706

Sections

1. Death, grief, funerals and feelings 5
2. Death of a parent 16
3. Death of a grandparent 28
4. Death of a sibling 52
5. Caregiver notes about the story books 58
6. Author and illustrator 60

INTRODUCTION

Adults who work with grieving children of all ages have a giant challenge. How can we help these children understand the feelings and emotions that come after the death of a loved one? How can we help them cope with the feelings of guilt and regret? How can we answer their questions in a kind, loving, honest way? How can we lead them into an understanding of the importance of talking about memories and sharing their feelings with others? How can we comfort them?

Adults who want to help are different in many ways. Some have had no training in counseling. Some have had a few hours of training to help them as facilitators in grief support programs. Some have university degrees in counseling. However, they all have a desire to help, a need for support materials as they help, and a desire for suggestions to use the support materials. Their main concern is to supply love and comfort to a child or group of children.

Some of the adults are also grieving. They, too, need help and comfort as they relate to family members and friends. They are striving to help themselves and others.

WHAT IS THE PURPOSE OF THIS BOOK?

This resource book has five major purposes:
1. Suggest specific Centering Corporation books for specific needs
2. Describe ways to use the suggested books with children
3. Provide directions for a follow-up activity that will help support the story book being used
4. Discuss ideas to tie together the content of the book and the follow-up activity
5. Share ideas for varied uses of the books within special settings

WHY ARE STORY BOOKS GOOD TOOLS TO USE IN GRIEF SUPPORT ACTIVITIES?

There are several reasons why story books are effective tools for working with children. Children love to hear stories and enjoy good illustrations. They can relate to characters and situations within a story and understand that others have had the same feelings and pain that they have.

Elementary school children are ready to use analogies. They can do inferential thinking based on what is happening in a story and what they know and are experiencing. Talking about a character in a story is often easier than talking about oneself. The discussion of characters and events in a story can gently lead the child into more personal conversation and sharing.

Death and grieving have special vocabularies. The funeral and burial have special vocabulary terms and concepts that are new to children. Using the vocabulary in a story can facilitate a child's understanding of the concepts that need to be understood when coping with grief. One example is being able to put a label on an emotion the child is experiencing.

Using a story book with a particular theme can facilitate the adult's attempts to present specific ideas in a focused way. Too often adults provide too many unrelated pieces of information. The child then fails to put what he has experienced into a clear picture, or to really understand what has been discussed and shared. The correct follow-up activity can also help the child tie the information together.

HOW IS THE RIGHT BOOK SELECTED FOR USE?

Following are some questions we must ask when selecting just the right book. Where are the children in the grief process? What do we see as the pressing needs of the children as they cope with grief? What do the children already know and understand about death? What questions are they asking? When and where will be the book be used? Who will guide the child as the book is used? Is a book worthy of the time to be spent using it? Are the formats of the book and its contents appropriate for the age and developmental characteristics of the children that you will be serving? This book suggests the appropriate age group for certain story books.

WHAT ARE SOME SUGGESTIONS FOR SHARING THE BOOK WITH CHILDREN?

Note: this book uses "children" but the material also applies for working with an individual child. The adult needs to be familiar with the book and its format. This book provides a summary of each story because the facilitator may not always have the opportunity to review the book before meeting with the children. In addition, you may be using a story book on multiple days by different facilitators. You can also review the summaries rather than the story books in group meetings for facilitators.

Study the pictures in the book carefully. How do the pictures add to or reinforce the story? Sometimes there are details in the pictures that are not in the story.

Introduce the book by sharing the characters and a brief introduction of the story problem. Help the children set purposes for listening. The ADULT should read the book with expression and with appropriate emotions. The children need to listen and become personally involved in the story. If a child is decoding and reading for an audience, the ideas of the story become secondary to the reading performance. If only one child is involved and the child is a good reader, some of the reading may be silent, or the child and adult can take turns reading.

While reading to a group, pause and give the children time to think about the text and the pictures. Where appropriate, this book recommends you read a specific story book in sections and discuss a section before reading the next section. This was done because the ideas in the story were developed in an important sequence. The parts of the story often build upon each other.

The attitude of the adult reading and guiding the discussion is contagious. If the adult is interested in the content of the story and expresses appropriate feelings and reactions, the children will also want to be involved in the story.

Watch the children as you read. If a child wants to comment about the pictures or a part of the story, you do not have to wait until the discussion time. There may be times when you can tell the children are anxious to ask questions. Be sure to provide time for this.

WHAT ARE SOME SUGGESTIONS FOR GUIDING THE DISCUSSION?

In some of the books, the pages are not numbered. In order to use the suggested questions, you will need to number the pages. For each story book, this book identifies the first page to number.

You are not expected to ask all of the suggested questions. Select questions that best fit the age of the children. The literal questions are there to provide building blocks for the inferential questions. Answers to literal questions are mere facts. Inferential questions require the children to relate personally to the story and are based on analogies. They require the children to draw conclusions. At times the adult will need to rephrase a question or to scaffold. Scaffolding is used when a partial answer is given. Ask questions like: "Can you tell us more?" "Do the rest of you agree with _____?" "Who would like to add to what has been said?" Scaffold questions can help children extend their thinking and personally relate to the story.

Each child who hears the story will find parts of the story that are more relevant. Pull the reticent, quiet child into the discussion by asking questions such as "_____, do you agree with _____?" "Would you like to add something?" Be careful not to let one or two children dominate the discussion.

Respect the responses of each child, and expect children in a group setting to do the same. Create a safe, warm environment for children to feel comfortable and share. Respect each child's privacy. Do not repeat things said by a child or use the child's name in sharing with others outside the group.

There will be occasions when a child does not have a lot of happy memories of the person who died. This child can build on the memories of loving friends and family members. Encourage these memories.

The reticent child may respond in a private conversation during the project time. Sometimes children who have had shared losses, such as a father, will share and enjoy an aside discussion during work/play time.

If you sense very special needs of a child during discussion time, visit with a counselor or parent and discuss ways to give that child some specific help.

THOUGHTS FROM THE AUTHOR

I sincerely hope that I have presented some food for thought, help for you as you serve people who are grieving, and encouragement for you as you face your challenge. We often tell the children we serve that they are special and that they are loved. You need to know the same things.

Your desire to serve others is appreciated. What you do is important as you help children and teens face their feelings and emotions. As you provide opportunities for these precious people to share their memories and ask questions, you can help the healing process begin in their lives. You have the opportunity to help these children grow up with healthy attitudes toward life and death. You will be changing lives. Along the way, your life will also be changed and blessed.

SECTION 1
USING STORYBOOKS TO EXPLAIN DEATH, GRIEF, FUNERALS, AND FEELINGS

The Healing Tree

By Kathleen Maresh Hemery

Illustrated by Kyra Teis

BOOK SUMMARY

Sammy and his grandmother Baba visit a big tree. The tree has a scar; bark is not growing on part of the trunk. Grandmother explains the scar by telling a story. When she was a girl the tree was in her yard. Her mother died and the grandmother ran to the swing in the tree and stayed there. A storm came and Grandmother's papa came and took her inside. A streak of lightening hit the tree and split it. A large branch fell off of the tree. Grandmother had lost something dear to her. The tree also lost part of itself.

Baba tells Sammy that she and the tree continued to live, but the scars are still there. Sammy and Baba swing together and soar into the air.

SUGGESTIONS FOR USE OF THE BOOK

The book has beautiful pictures that share the seasons of life for the grandmother and the tree. The love of the father and the grandmother bring comfort to the grandmother as a girl.

Read slowly and give children time to study the beautiful pictures. Ask the children what they think the word "healing" means. Ask if one of them might have a scar that is left from a sore that healed. The understanding of the words "healing" and "scar" needs to be developed. Show the picture on the front cover and explain that as the story is shared they will find why the tree got its name. Share the picture on page 2 and introduce Sammy and Baba Marta. The word "Baba" means grandmother.

Where are the two? Tell the children that Baba Marta sat in a swing, under the same tree, when she was a girl. "Let's read and find out more about Baba Marta and the "Healing Tree".

QUESTIONS TO GUIDE THE DISCUSSION

Pages 1-4.
1. Why was Baba Marta sad as she and Sammy sat in the swing?
2. What did Sammy notice about the tree?
3. How had Baba Marta felt when her mother died?
4. Why do you think she ran from her father and went to the tree?
5. Do you remember who told you about the death of your loved one? What did you do?
6. Is it okay to want to be alone for a while?
7. Where do you go to be alone?

Pages 5-8.
1. What memories did Baba Marta have of her mother and the tree? Were these happy memories?
2. The tree reminded Baba Marta of her mother.
3. What reminds you of your loved one?
4. Is there a place that makes you feel close to your loved one?
5. What is that place, and why is it special?

Pages 9-14.
1. What happened to the tree the evening that Baba Marta was told about her mother's death?
2. Why was the storm like death? What did it kill?
3. Who came and comforted Baba Marta? How did he comfort her?
4. Is there someone who has comforted you and made you feel better?
5. Why did Baba Marta and Papa feel like the tree?
6. Do you feel like part of you is missing? Explain.

Pages 15-19.
1. Why did Baba Marta say that the tree would always have a scar? How are you like that tree?
2. How did Baba Marta heal?
3. Why was a new swing put in the tree? Who enjoyed the new swing?
4. How do you think Baba Marta and Sammy felt as they kicked their feet and went high in the swing?
5. Did the story have a happy ending? Why?
6. Do you think your story will have a happy ending some day? Why?
7. What is your "healing place"?

FOLLOW-UP ACTIVITY

☞ The children can create trees by gluing autumn leaves on a trunk that has been glued or drawn on a sheet of double sized manila or construction paper. The children can draw a swing under the tree. Label the picture "THE HEALING TREE". Older children can write special memories around the tree. Younger children can talk and the facilitator can record their memories.

☞ An optional idea for children who are old enough to write would be to create a booklet made of large leaf-shaped pages. The children can draw and label a picture of a special memory.

☞ If several children are in the group, end by asking the children to turn to neighbors and share some of the memories. Children who volunteer could then share with the entire group.

☞ Remind the children that these memories can help bring healing. The scar will remain, but the healing can come.

Lucy Lettuce

By Patrick Loring and Joy Johnson

Illustrated by Caroline Crider

BOOK SUMMARY

The story tells of a seed that grows into a round head of lettuce. She moves to a refrigerator where she has friends. Sometimes she is in the light; sometimes she is in the dark.

One day, Lucy is taken from the refrigerator and her heart is cut out. She is smashed on a counter. She goes on with her life. Her tears flow like water. She is put into a salad spinner. She feels mixed up and as if she is going crazy. The spinning stops and Lucy sees light. She is moved to a board where she sees old and new friends. She knows her life will never be the same. She might be tossed again.

Grief can be compared to what Lucy Lettuce has experienced. After her experience, she finds a new normal and is able to reach out to others.

SUGGESTIONS FOR USE OF THE BOOK

The book includes plans for creating a salad while reading the book.. Caregivers and facilitators who work with adult, teens and older elementary children could use the book and the hands-on experience. The salad making instructions include the ingredients and a script. Elementary children would benefit from hearing the book read before or after the salad making.

Number the pages, beginning with the first full page picture.

A summary of each page displays in a dark band across the top of each page. That summary, or the one shared above, might introduce the salad making experience. An adult who is involved in the counseling session would enjoy having a copy of the book to use at home.

QUESTIONS TO GUIDE THE DISCUSSION

Part 1. Happy days in Lucy's life, pages 1-4.
1. What did the authors mean when they said that Lucy had "self-esteem"?
2. Why do you think Lucy liked her home in the refrigerator?
3. Could the "dark times" in the refrigerator be a foreshadowing of coming events in Lucy's life? Why?
4. Did you have some "hints" that your life was going to change?

Part 2. Lucy's life in the spinner, pages 5-8.
1. Do you remember the minute that your life changed? How did you know?
2. What does it mean when we say someone is in "shock"? How does this person act?
3. Did you act this way when you realized that the one you loved had died?
4. How was Lucy tough? Have you been tough in some way?
5. Why did the people around Lucy not know that her heart was torn out?

Part 3. Lucy becomes a new person, pages 9-13.
1. Is some light beginning to come into your life? What has brought that light?
2. How can you have a "new normal"?
3. How did Lucy's friends bring her comfort? Who are some friends that have brought some comfort to you?
4. What does spice do to food? How can we have new spice in our lives?
5. Lucy had a new part that replaced her old heart. The one she loved lived there.
6. What does this mean?
7. What does it mean to "nurture" others? What can you do to help others who have, or will, lose a loved one to death?

FOLLOW-UP ACTIVITY

☞ Elementary children could make their own salads after they hear and talk about the story. Use commercial wipes to allow them to wash their hands. Use the lettuce head to demonstrate the removal of the heart and the spinning.

☞ You can provide pre-prepared peppers and tomatoes. Provide a choice of salad dressings. You could also provide croutons and shredded cheese to add "spice" to the salads the children will prepare. Guide the children as they discuss each ingredient. Suggest that they have prepared a salad that can them understand how they feel and bring enjoyment. They are not going to change their feelings overnight, but new friends and new things can help them find a new "normal".

☞ As the children enjoy their salads, suggest that they might share what they talked about with their family members. They might make, or help make, salad for a meal and tell their family the story of Lucy lettuce. Encourage the children to make a new friend by trying one new ingredient in their salad.

☞ Encourage the children to talk about their friends and to encourage them to make new friends. If the children are served by a program that serves adults and children, the session shared in the book could be used with all family members in their small group settings. This would facilitate further discussion of family group ideas at a later time.

Ragtail Remembers

By Liz Duckworth

Illustrated by Jeffrey P. Barnes

BOOK SUMMARY

This delightful story of a mouse who has a friend who dies can be used with preschool and elementary age children. The pictures are large and colorful and help tell the story. This book emphasizes the importance of friends who care when we are sad. The loss of a pet, or a personal friend, can be explored by using the book in a one-on-one or a small group setting.

The last page of the book includes a list of feelings and emotions that are normal. Ways to cope with these feelings are shared. The importance of sharing is explored.

SUGGESTIONS FOR USE OF THE BOOK

If you use the book with preschool children, you will want to select questions that are suitable for younger children. Base the discussion for these younger children on the pictures and talk about what is happening in the pictures.

Number the pages, beginning with the first full page picture. The story falls into four parts. Give the children quiet time to think and study the pictures. Accept comments and questions as you read.

Use the picture on page 1 to introduce Ragtail. Ask the children to talk about what he is doing. Explain that he is looking for a friend, Old Tim, a cat. Ask them to listen carefully and find out what has happened to Old Tim and what Ragtail does when he hears the boy and man talking.

QUESTIONS TO GUIDE THE DISCUSSION

Part 1. Ragtail searches for Old Tim, pages 1-8.
1. What things did the two friends do together?
2. What did Frazzle do when Ragtail tried to ask about Old Tim?
3. How is Ragtail beginning to feel? Why did he shiver?
4. How did Ragtail feel after he wished and Old Tim did not appear? What did he decide to do to make Old Tim come back?

Part 2. Ragtail learns about death, pages 9-10.
1. Why is Frazzle serious when he answers Ragtail's questions about death?
2. Ragtail was heartsick. What does this mean? Have you felt this way?
3. What made Ragtail's heart feel better? What did frazzle do as Ragtail cried?
4. Do you think Razzle is a friend to Ragtail? Why?

Part 3. Old Tim is buried, pages 11-14.
1. Who buried Old Tim? How did they bury Old Tim?
2. What did the boy and man do after they buried Old Tim? What is this memorial service called?
3. What did Ragtail do after the man and boy left? When people talk about a friend after the burial, the talking is called a eulogy. What did Ragtail include in his eulogy?
4. What did Frazzle do for Old Tim? What did Frazzle promise Ragtail? Why?

Part 4. Remembering Old Tim, pages 15-20.
1. How did Frazzle continue to help Ragtail? Do you have a friend who has helped you as you have felt the sadness of death?
2. How did Frazzle use the leaf to teach Ragtail about death?
3. How had Ragtail changed? Have you changed because of the death of a loved one?
4. Why do you think Ragtail put the dead leaf on Old Tim's grave?
5. Did Ragtail stop hurting? What does Ragtail still do at times?
6. Did playing with a new friend help Ragtail? Did the new friend really take the place of his old friend?
7. Is it okay to find new friends?

FOLLOW-UP ACTIVITY

☞ Use brightly colored autumn leaves, or artificial leaves in the making of a place mat, or table mat.

☞ Each child will need two pieces of waxed paper, some colored leaves, some pieces of colored string, and some shaved pieces of old crayons. The facilitator will need paper towels, an iron and a large towel to use as an ironing board.

☞ Use the following steps to make a mat:
1. Lay the towel on a table top, away from the table where the children are working. Plug the iron in and heat it. Be sure that an adult is with the iron at all times.
2. Give each child a piece of waxed paper,
3. Have the child arrange leaves, string, and shaved crayon on the waxed paper.
4. The child brings his waxed paper creation to the person who is by the iron.
5. The child lays the second sheet of waxed paper on top of the first sheet.
6. Cove the two pieces of waxed paper with paper towels.
7. With the help of the adult, the child irons the paper towels to seal the arrangement between the sheets of waxed paper. Only one child should be near the iron.

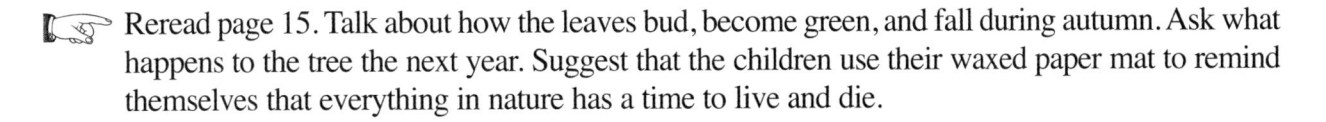

☞ Reread page 15. Talk about how the leaves bud, become green, and fall during autumn. Ask what happens to the tree the next year. Suggest that the children use their waxed paper mat to remind themselves that everything in nature has a time to live and die.

I Know I Made It Happen

By Lynn Bennett Blackburn

Illustrated by Glenda Dietrich

BOOK SUMMARY

The book shares several bad things that a child feel is his or her fault. A sister falls from a tree. A brother gets sick. A grandmother dies. In each case, the child shares reasons why he is to blame. There is always an adult there to help. The account of the grandma's funeral and the tribute by the child is a highlight of the book. The last part of the book is based on divorce. Again the child feels guilt. In each incident, clues for understanding the feeling of guilt are provided by a loving family member. The pictures add greatly to the book. These are crayon drawings that use vivid and dark colors to convey the emotions being experienced by the child.

SUGGESTIONS FOR USE OF THE BOOK

You can read this book to children in sections, based on the events discussed. Provide time for the children to think about and discuss the crayon drawings. What emotions do the colors elicit? Give the children opportunities to share any feelings of guilt that they may have. The pages are not numbered. Begin numbering with the first page of text.

QUESTIONS TO GUIDE THE DISCUSSION

Part 1. A fall from a tree, pages 1-2.
1. Why was the child mad at his sister? What did he tell his sister?
2. Do you think the child really wanted the sister to break a leg?
3. What accident did Grandma ask the child to remember?
4. Why do you think the grandma suggested that the child play a game with his sister?

Part 2. A brother becomes ill, pages 3-6.
1. What were the child and the brother doing together?
2. Why did the child get mad at the brother?
3. What did he tell his brother? Do you think he really meant what he said?
4. What did Mom say made the brother sick? Do you think she was right?
5. Why did the boy feel left out? (Attention given to sick brother, not feeling noticed, feeling guilty.)

6. How did the child help his brother and himself?
7. Does saying, "I'm sorry" usually help?

Part 3. Grandma dies, pages 7-10.
1. Why did the boy feel guilty about his grandma's death?
2. Why do you think the child was scared?
3. What did his mother tell him about Grandma's death?

Part 4. The funeral, pages 11-14.
1. What did the boy and his mother tie to his grandma's coffin?
2. What did they boy say as he dropped the petals of the daisies?
3. Was this a good way for the child to tell Grandma that she was loved?
4. What happened to the balloon when it got flat?
5. Why do you think the child and mother will go back to the grave and take daisies?

Part 5. A divorce, pages 15-18.
1. Why does the child feel that he caused the divorce? Did he?
2. What did his Aunt Sarah explain to him?
3. What was the boy really worried about?
4. Did telling the parents that he was afraid that they would stop loving him help?
5. What did the parents tell the child?
6. Does talking make you feel better?

Part 6. The conclusion, pages 19-21.
1. Why is it hard to understand why some things happen?
2. Is there always someone to blame?
3. Do your wishes and words make bad things happen?
4. What have we learned about people?
5. What have we learned about how we can feel better?

FOLLOW-UP ACTIVITY

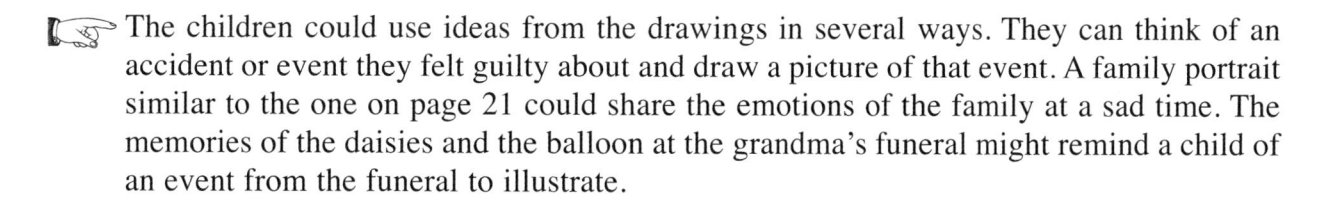

☞ The children could use ideas from the drawings in several ways. They can think of an accident or event they felt guilty about and draw a picture of that event. A family portrait similar to the one on page 21 could share the emotions of the family at a sad time. The memories of the daisies and the balloon at the grandma's funeral might remind a child of an event from the funeral to illustrate.

☞ Take time at the end of the session to invite the children to share their pictures and comments about the pictures. Remind them that bad words and wishes do not make bad things happen. Ask them to share something that they learned that can help them feel happier in the coming days. Remind them that are adults who love them and who are always willing to listen.

Tell Me Papa

By Joy and Dr. Marvin Johnson
Illustrated by Ann Catherine Blake

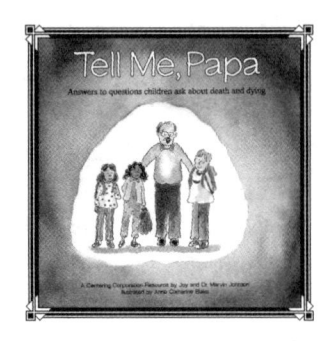

BOOK SUMMARY

Papa talks to three children and describes death and what happens when someone dies. He uses the analogy of an apple peel, a peanut shell, and an empty school to describe the body. The role of the funeral director and the funeral home are shared. What happens to the body and the preparation for the funeral are discussed. Visitation at the funeral home and the home are included. The purposes for the visits are given. The funeral and what happens after the funeral are discussed in a clear, thoughtful manner. The trip to the cemetery and what happens at the grave site are included. The option of cremation is shared and explained. The book ends with Papa encouraging the children to ask questions about things that they don't understand.

SUGGESTION FOR USE OF THE BOOK

This beautiful book can be used in several ways. The book can used in its entirety or in part. A grief support program could use it for more than one session. The pictures are great and can help guide the discussion.

QUESTIONS TO GUIDE THE DISCUSSION

Part 1. The finality of death, pages 1-6.
1. What are some examples of things in nature that die? (falling leaves, cycle of butterfly, etc.)
2. How did the children feel about Percy Grey-Paws? (Use the picture on p.4 as the different emotions are discussed.)
3. Why are our feelings real and important?
4. What happens to someone when they die? (Use the pictures on pages 5 and 6 as you talk about this.)

Part 2. The funeral home and getting ready for the funeral, pages 7-12.
1. What does a funeral director do? (Use picture on page 8.)
2. What happens to the body when it gets to the funeral home?
3. What is a casket? (Use picture on page 10.)
4. What is true of the body in the casket? How can seeing the body in the casket help us say good-bye? (Use picture on page 12.)

Part 3. The funeral, pages 13-16.
1. Why do people come to the home of the one who died? (Use picture on page 14.)
2. Why do they bring flowers and food? How may the people treat a child?
3. What happens at the funeral? (Use picture on page 16.)
4. Why is crying OK?

Part 4. The trip to the cememtery and the grave, pages 17-20.
1. What happens when the funeral is over? (Use picture on pages 17 and 18.)
2. What is seen at the cemetery?
3. What can happen after the casket is covered with earth? (Use picture on page 20.)
4. Why do people return to visit the grave?

Part 5. Cremation, pages 21-22.
1. What is a crematorium?
2. What do the ashes look like?
3. What can be done with the ashes? (Use picture on page 22.)

Part 6. Conclusion and visit to Percy Grey-Paws grave, pages 23-26.
1. Why does Papa encourage the children to ask questions?
2. Do you have questions you need to ask?
3. What are the children doing? (Use picture on page 25.)
4. What do the thought balloons tell us about the children? (Use picture on page 26.)

FOLLOW-UP ACTIVITY

☞ Provide time for children to ask their personal questions.

☞ Children can draw pictures of things they remember about the funeral or the trip to the cemetery.

☞ Children can make tissue paper flowers to take to the cemetery.

☞ A funeral home director could visit a grief support group. Remind children that saying good-bye is important, but talking about their memories will also continue to be important.

SECTION 2
USING STORYBOOKS TO EXPLAIN GRIEF AND LOSS AFTER THE DEATH OF A PARENT

Sam's Dad Died

By Margaret H. Holmes

Illustrated by Susan Aitken

BOOK SUMMARY

Sam had the same name as his father. His father had told him that the name told people who they were. Sam wishes that he could talk to his dad. Sam and his mother enjoy talking and remembering funny things that happened when they were together. There are times when Sam wants to act like a baby and times when he wants to be big like his dad was. He gets comfort and enjoys talking to a friend who also lost his dad to death. Sometimes Sam cries and feels embarrassed. He feels better after he cries.

Schoolwork is hard for Sam. He tries to do his best work. Even though he is grieving, Sam enjoys playing with his friends. The last page shares how Sam felt when his dad was alive. Sam still feels loved by his dad.

SUGGESTIONS FOR USE OF THE BOOK

You can use the book with one child or a group of children. Number the pages, beginning with the first page of illustration and text. Read each page slowly. Stop and give quiet time as children study the pictures and think. Read one page at a time and use the discussion questions to guide the discussion. Encourage children to share, but be gentle in eliciting their responses. Sometimes a child who has not participated can become a part of the discussion if you call the child by name and request a response.

Introduce Sam to the children by sharing his picture. Explain that Sam is going to tell them about his dad who has died. Suggest that they listen carefully to discover how Sam is feeling.

QUESTIONS FOR GUIDING THE DISCUSSION

Page 1:
How are names important? Is your name important? Why?

Page 2:
Do you worry about making someone else sad? If so, who? Do you think that person might be wishing for someone to talk to about the loved one that both of you are missing? What might you talk about?

Page 3:
How do you and your family members share memories? Would you like to share a memory with us?

Page 4:
Is there some way that you would be like to be like your loved one who died? What did you admire about that person?

Page 5:
Do you have a friend who has also had a death in his or her family? Have you and that friend talked about death? Did that talk help you feel better? Why?

Page 6:
Do you sometimes feel like crying? Is that okay? Should you be ashamed to cry?

Page 7:
Do you find it difficult to keep your mind on school tasks? What are some things that can help? (You might discuss studying with a friend, reading aloud, asking for help, talking to the school counselor, and tutoring sessions.)

Page 8:
Do you have a special place where you go to be by yourself? Would you like to tell us about that place? What do you do there?

Page 9:
What do you and your friends do together that is fun? Should you feel guilty when you have fun and laugh? Would your loved one want you to be happy?

Page 10:
Do you remember how you felt when you were with the one who died? Is there a special time that you remember and could share? When did you feel loved? Can you still feel and know that you are loved?

FOLLOW-UP ACTIVITY

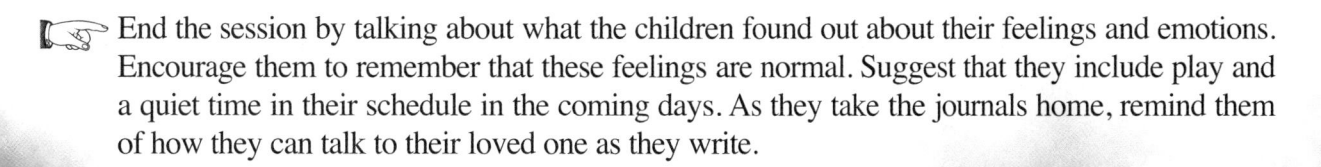

- A small spiral notebook or pad could become a journal. Encourage each child to write in that journal each day in his quiet place. The first entry can be written during the session.

- A picture of a favorite memory could be drawn on the first page of the journal, before the written entry is made. If there is time, provide a game for the children to play and enjoy together.

- End the session by talking about what the children found out about their feelings and emotions. Encourage them to remember that these feelings are normal. Suggest that they include play and a quiet time in their schedule in the coming days. As they take the journals home, remind them of how they can talk to their loved one as they write.

Molly's Mom Died

By Margaret M. Holmes
Illustrated by Susan Aitken

BOOK SUMMARY

The story is told in first person by Molly. She recalls the ways she tried to make her mother happy during her mother's illness. She shares her feelings of fear and anger. She feels different from others and is very lonely. Her emotions vary from tears to laughter. Schoolwork is hard for her. She gets comfort from memories of things that she and her mother did together, such as talking and laughing. Her mother had told her of the love she had for her daughter. It is that memory which sustains Molly.

SUGGESTIONS FOR USE OF THE BOOK

Number the pages, beginning with the first page of real text. Read a page and use the discussion question for that page. Move slowly and give the children time to study the pictures and think. Do not be afraid of short periods of quiet time. Some of the best conversation often comes after these quiet times. Encourage all of the children to participate in some way. You might want to call a child by name and ask what he is thinking, or if she agrees with a statement someone else made.

The book may be used with an individual child or a group of children. Make the children comfortable. Wait until they are ready to listen. Show a picture of Molly and explain that she is going to tell them about her mother who died. Mention that they will understand what Molly says. Suggest that they think about how they feel like Molly.

QUESTIONS FOR GUIDING THE DISCUSSION

Page 1:
How did Molly get her name? Who gave you your name? Were you named after a member of your family?

Page 2:
Did you get to help your loved one while he, or she, was ill? What did you do? How did you feel when you were able to help?

Page 3:
How can someone feel both grown-up and small? When do you feel grown-up? When do you feel small? Which is the best feeling? Is it okay for a child to feel small?

Page 4:
Where do you go for a quiet time? What do you think about?

Page 5:
Do you think your friends understand when you cry? Why not? Is it okay to cry? (Help the children understand that crying is normal and can help them feel better.)

Page 6:
What special things do you and your friends do? Is it okay to laugh and have a good time? (Help the children understand that they should not feel guilty when they have a good time.) Do you think your loved one who is no longer with you would want you to have a good time? Can you remember a time when you saw that person pleased because you were having a good time?

Page 7:
Why is it hard to do your best at school? Can one of you share something that seems to help you do better at school? (This might include studying with a friend, reading aloud, asking the teacher for help, visiting the school counselor, or attending tutoring sessions.)

Page 8:
What special things did you and your loved one do together? How do you know you were loved? Do you think grown-ups still think about how their parents loved them?

FOLLOW-UP ACTIVITY

- The children might draw pictures of activities they shared with their loved one. These pictures could be left in their quiet place and become a part of their thinking time. They can add other pictures later. The pictures can be placed in a folder.

- Another activity might be the writing in a journal kept in the quiet place. The first entry of the journal could be written during this session. The journal goes home with the child.

- Provide a game time that allows the children to laugh and enjoy each other.

- End the session by asking children if they have comments about any of the things discussed. Do they have a better understanding of how they feel and how to accept those feelings? Ask some of the children to share what they plan to do during the week to use some of the things discussed in this session.

The Snowman

By Robin Helene Vogel
Illustrated by Caroline Christian

BOOK SUMMARY

Two brothers have lost a father to death. The brothers build a snowman and begin to question and talk about the death of the father. The older brother becomes very angry and destroys the snowman. They cry together and begin to talk of happy memories. The snowman is repaired and the boys feel better.

A good summary of the book is found on the back cover. "The Snowman was the first Tommy and Buddy build since Dad died. They had Dad's old pipe. They found his favorite scarf. His hat was ready and so were the big buttons for the eyes. And the two brothers were ready, too - ready to talk about how Dad died and what his death meant to them.

Tommy and Buddy talk about feelings real to all of us. Then, as the snowman is finished and they head inside, Buddy experiences a trick of the light from the moon. Or was it?"

SUGGESTIONS FOR USE OF THE BOOK

You can use this book with one child, a small group, or a class of students. The pictures are large enough that a teacher could share them while reading. If a child in the classroom has lost a parent, the book could help the classmates understand the emotions and feelings of the one who has had a death in the family. If used with an entire classroom, the questions may need to be adapted to fit the group. The use of the book with parents could help the surviving parent understand some of the behavior of the child who has lost a parent in death.

Share the front cover. Tell the children that this special snowman is going to teach two brothers some important lessons. Introduce the brothers by using page 4.

Tommy is the older brother. Buddy is the younger brother. Suggest that they listen carefully and find out what happens to the snowman. They are to think about the lessons the snowman teaches the boys.

QUESTIONS FOR GUIDING THE DISCUSSION

Page 5
1. Does playtime with a friend or a family member make you feel better? Why?

Page 7
1. Even while playing, Buddy could not forget about his father's death. What question did Buddy ask?
2. Why do you think he asked a question that he knew the answer to?

Page 8
1. Tom's voice changed when Buddy asked his question again. Why?
2. Are you sometimes cross with a family member or friend?
3. Why do you think you act this way? Does this mean that you do not love that person?
4. What was Tom mad about when he kicked the snowman? Was he wrong to feel this way?

Page 10
1. What reminder did Buddy give Tommy about their dad's love?
2. Why did Tommy understand how his friend Kevin felt?
3. Why was Tommy blaming himself for his father's death?

Page 13
1. What did the boys do as they cried? What do you think this meant?
2. This was the first time Tommy had cried. Why? Is it okay to cry?
3. Buddy is worried about his mom. Why?

Page 15
1. How can other family members help? Who are your other family members?
2. Why do you think Tommy wanted to repair the snowman himself?
3. Why did Tommy let Buddy replace the eye?

Page 17
1. What did the boys discover about the scarf and pipe?
2. What happy memories came to the boys?

Page 18
1. Do you think the snowman really winked?
2. What did Buddy think when he saw the snowman wink?
3. Do you think the brothers felt better as they went inside?

FOLLOW-UP ACTIVITY

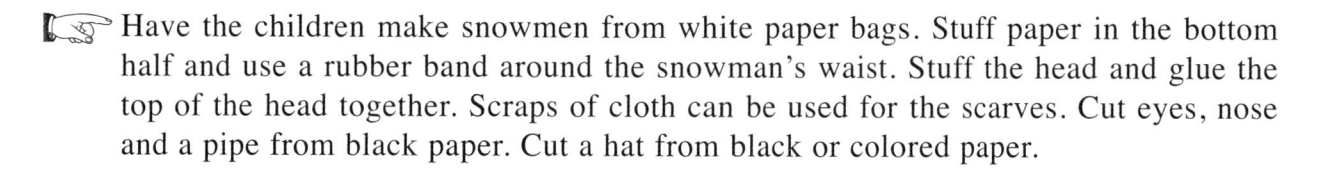

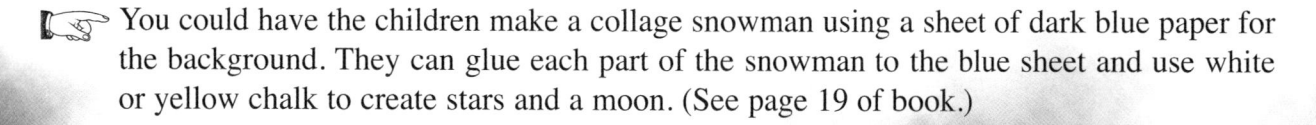

☞ Have the children make snowmen from white paper bags. Stuff paper in the bottom half and use a rubber band around the snowman's waist. Stuff the head and glue the top of the head together. Scraps of cloth can be used for the scarves. Cut eyes, nose and a pipe from black paper. Cut a hat from black or colored paper.

☞ You could have the children make a collage snowman using a sheet of dark blue paper for the background. They can glue each part of the snowman to the blue sheet and use white or yellow chalk to create stars and a moon. (See page 19 of book.)

☞ The children can display their snowmen on a table or hold them as the session ends. Remind the children that you want them to think about the lessons the snowman taught the boys. Some of the comments might be about the feeling of guilt and anger. These feelings are normal. Accept any logical response from a child. End the session by asking if one of these lessons might help the children. Give opportunities for a few personal responses. Suggest that they take their snowmen home and put them where they can be seen. They can share the snowman and its lessons with other family members.

Sunflowers & Rainbows for Tia

By Alesia Alexander Greene
Illustrated by Clarissa Love

BOOK SUMMARY

The book begins with an introduction of Tia, her twin brothers, and her parents. The father becomes ill. One night after the children have gone to sleep, the grandmother comes and takes them home with her. The next day the children learn that their father has died. Tia runs out of the house into her grandfather's sunflowers. There she cries. The mother and the children select a coffin and help plan the funeral. Neighbors and friends come to show that they care and to bring food. The day of the funeral is rainy and dismal. As the family leaves the cemetery, Tia sees a beautiful rainbow. She thinks it is a sign from her father as he smiles down at them. The rainbow comforts the family.

SUGGESTIONS FOR USE OF THE BOOK

The book is a little long for younger elementary age children. The caregiver could use the pictures and tell the story in fewer words. The pictures add to the story and can be used during the discussion.

This is a good book for a counselor to use with a child who attended a funeral. When only one child is involved, you can carefully choose a few questions for discussion. With a group of children include more questions. This allows more individual children to respond.

Number the pages, beginning with the first page of text. Because of the length of the story, the book has been divided into sections for reading and discussion. Read with expression. Give the children time to comment about pictures or events in the story. Many children have questions about the things that happen before, during and after a funeral.

Introduce the book by reading the first page and sharing the picture of the children. Share that things in the family are about to change.

QUESTIONS FOR GUIDING THE DISCUSSION

Part 1. The night of the death, pages 2-6
1. What were the noises that Tia heard during the night?
2. Why do you think she was afraid?
3. Why do you think Granny took the children to her home?
4. Why did the sunflowers not raise their faces as the children went with Granny to her car?
5. Why did Tia run to her grandfather's sunflowers? What did she do there?

Part 2. The children and others learn about the death, pages 7-12
1. What things had Tia thought about as she thought of her mother?
2. What did Jay not understand about death?
3. What did Mama explain about death?
4. Why was Tia mad? Have you felt mad about the death of your loved one?
5. Why did Tia not enjoy the food?
6. Did the people and their gifts help Tia? How did she feel as she saw and listened to the people?
7. People laughed and cried. Why do you think they did this?
8. What things did Tia worry about as she thought about her daddy not being with her any more?

Part 3. Planning the funeral, pages 13-16
1. What is a funeral?
2. How did Tia's mother say each funeral was different?
3. What is a casket? Do you remember your loved one's casket?
4. What is a funeral spray? Do you remember the spray on your loved one's casket?
5. Why did Tia think of sunflowers?
6. What did the children do to help plan the funeral? What did they put in the casket? Why do you think they did this?

Part 4. The funeral, pages 17-20
1. How did the children dress for the funeral? Why was the color yellow important to them?
2. What did Grandfather mean when he said that Tia's daddy's memory was big enough for all of them to share?
3. What did Tia take to the funeral and why?
4. How did the weather fit the day?
5. Tia cried when her grandfather read the poem that she and the twins had selected. Why did she feel good and cry at the same time when the poem was read?
6. What happened on the way to the cemetery? What did Tia think the rainbow was?
7. Do you have some special memories of the funeral for your family member?

FOLLOW-UP ACTIVITY

☞ The last page of the book includes instructions to plant sunflowers as a memorial. The facilitator might share the seeds and the instructions given by the author. The activity could be a family project.

☞ Page 18 of the book is a beautiful picture of the sunflowers and the rainbow. Use a large sheet of manila or drawing paper for the children to draw large sunflowers. They can glue actual sunflower seeds or other seeds in the centers of the flowers. The rainbow can be done with water colors or crayons. Display the picture in the book for children to see as they work.

☞ Close the session by talking about the follow-up project or projects. Provide some time for children to ask any questions they might have about funerals. Some of the children may not have attended the funeral of their family member. These children may have questions that only another family member can answer.

☞ Ask the children why the rainbow appears in the sky. It signals that a time of rain is over. There will be some sunshine. Talk about how death is like a time of rain.

The Brightest Star

By Kathleen Maresh Hemerey

Illustrated by Ron Boldt

BOOK SUMMARY

Molly begins her story by sharing memories of things that she and her parents did at the beach. Her mother becomes ill and spends time in the hospital. Molly visits her mother. One day her dad comes home and tells Molly that her mother has died. Molly screams at her dad and cries. He holds her and tells her that they are going to be sad, scared and angry, but they will still be a family.

When Molly returns to school, her teacher asks the class to draw family portraits for parent night. Molly does not draw and decides that she will not attend the special night at school. Her teacher suggests that Molly take the paper for the picture home and talk to her dad. Molly is afraid that the picture will make her dad sad.

Dad takes Molly to the beach. They look at the stars. Dad suggests that the biggest star can remind them of Molly's mother. Molly does not have to forget her mother. Molly decides what she will put in her picture.

SUGGESTIONS FOR USE OF THE BOOK

The illustrations include drawings and photographs. These can add to the understanding of the story. Show the front cover of the book. Ask the child what the picture represents. Explain that the "biggest star" is going to become very important to Molly and her dad. Introduce Molly and her dad by sharing the picture on page 3. Tell the children that Molly has just received some sad news. Suggest that they listen carefully and find out what happened.

QUESTIONS FOR GUIDING THE DISCUSSION

Page 1.
1. What did Molly and her parents do at the beach?
2. Do you have special memories of a vacation or trip that you could share?

Pages 2-3.
1. Why do you think Molly's mother was glad that Molly visited her at the hospital?
2. Do you think it was easy for Molly to see her mother in the hospital? Why?
3. Why did Molly yell at her dad? Was she really mad at him, or at what he told her?
4. How did Molly's dad comfort her?

Pages 4-7.
1. Why do you suppose Molly was glad to get back to school?
2. Why did Molly not want to draw a portrait of her family?
3. Have you had a sad experience at school after the death of your loved one? Could you share that experience?
4. Do you worry about making others sad if you talk about your loved one? Is crying a bad thing to do?
5. Why do you think Ms. Bayer suggested that Molly include her grandmother in the portrait?
6. Why did Molly not want to do this? Can a grandmother really take the place of a mother?
7. How do we know that Ms. Bayer understood how Molly felt?

Pages 8-10.
1. Why did Molly think it would not be fair to her dad for her to pretend she was sick?
2. How did Dad know that Molly was upset?
3. Are there times when you know that members of your family are upset? What can you do to help them?
4. Where did Dad suggest that he and Molly go? Why?
5. What did Molly and Dad do at the beach?
6. Why do you think Dad suggested that the biggest star be a reminder of Molly's mother?
7. What do you think Molly will draw on her paper? Do you think she and Dad will go to parent night?
8. Will he recognize her drawing?
9. Is there something special that reminds you of your loved one? Why does it remind you of your loved one?

FOLLOW-UP ACTIVITY

☞ The children might make believe that they are Molly and draw the picture for parent night. The picture might be of Molly and Dad with a big star that includes the picture of Molly's mom.

☞ Another option would be for the students to use the ideas from the book but do a portrait of their family. The portraits could be mounted inside frames made of colored paper.

☞ Another option would be to cover a large cardboard star with foil and paste a picture of the loved one onto the star. The children could hang silver ribbon streamers from the star.

☞ Use the last minutes of the session to allow the children to share and talk about their portraits. Suggest that they display the portrait at home for their families to enjoy.

☞ Remind the children that they are still part of a family. It is okay to love others, like a grandma. The memories of the loved one can provide comfort. The love of those persons can continue to live in their hearts.

SECTION 3
USING STORYBOOKS TO EXPLAIN GRIEF AND LOSS AFTER THE DEATH OF A GRANDPARENT

Finding Grandpa Everywhere

By John Hodge

Illustrated by Susan Aitken

BOOK SUMMARY

A young boy is told by his parents that they have "lost" his grandpa. The boy remembers the time that he got lost in the mall. He is anxious to get to his grandpa's home and find him.

When the boy and his parents get to the home of the grandparents, there are many people in the house. None of the people seem to be searching for Grandpa. Everyone is dressed like they are going to church. Some of the people are crying. A lady tells him she is sorry that his grandpa died. The boy understands what has happened. He visits the backyard to look at Grandpa's garden. The garden is dead looking.

The young child returns to the house and finds his grandma and sits in her lap. His grandma explains that the grandpa will be buried. The young child tells his grandma that not all of his grandpa will be buried, only his body. He remembers that his grandpa told him to put a little of himself in all that he did. He reminds his grandma that Grandpa did a lot in the garden. Part of Grandpa was still there. The grandma asks her grandson to help her plant the tomato plants that Grandpa was going to plant. Helping with the tomato plants made the young child feel better.

SUGGESTIONS FOR USE OF THE BOOK

The beautiful pictures can be used to help tell the story. The book could also be used by a parent or grandparent with a child who has had a grandparent die.

If the book is used with one child, you can turn the questions into a conversation. If there are several children, elicit responses from as many as will share. You will need to number the pages of the book. Begin numbering with the first full-page picture.

Use the front cover to introduce the young child. Explain that the child is going to tell the story. Read the name of the book. Share the fact that the garden and the tomato plants remind the boy of his grandpa. Ask them to listen to find other things that remind the storyteller of his grandpa.

The story is told in five parts. Read the story parts and use some of the questions to elicit comments. Encourage the children to ask questions and share their personal comments.

QUESTIONS FOR GUIDING THE DISCUSSION

Part 1. The young child gets lost, pages 1-2.
1. Why was the day the boy got lost a scary one for his mother?
2. How did the boy feel when he realized he was lost?
3. Have you ever been lost? When? Where? How were you found?

Part 2. The young child looks for his grandpa, pages 3-6.
1. What did the boy think about on the way to his grandparent's home?
2. Share the picture on page 4. Why is the swing empty? What was written on Grandpa's hat?
3. Why is the boy looking under the table?
4. Why does he want to help his grandpa?

Part 3. The young child realizes his grandpa is dead, pages 7-8.
1. Why did the boy leave the kitchen?
2. Why did the stump remind the boy of his grandpa? Is there something that reminds you of your loved one who died? What?
3. What advice had the grandpa given the boy? Do you think that was good advice?
4. How can you put a part of everything into what you do?

Part 4. The young child and his grandma, pages 9-10.
1. Why did the boy put his grandpa's hat on his head? Is there something that your loved one wore that you would like to wear? What?
2. What question did the boy ask his grandma? What was her answer?
3. What did the boy mean when he said that not all of Grandpa would be buried?

Part 5. The young child finds a way to help his grandma, pages 11-12.
1. What did the young child share with his grandma about Grandpa?
2. What did the young child mean when he said that when she wanted to talk to Grandpa, she should look around her?
3. What did grandma ask her grandson to do?
4. Why was planting the tomatoes so important for both the young child and his grandma?
5. Grandma was sad, but she was also glad. Can that be true? How?
6. Can you think of something that you are glad about that is connected to the death of a family member?

FOLLOW-UP ACTIVITY

☞ Have the children personalize a coat hanger as a gift for a family member. Each child can trace the inner edges of the hanger on a piece of light-colored poster board or heavy paper.

☞ Decorate the traced part with "I (heart) (name)." Decorate the background with drawings. of things that remind the child of a family member living or dead.

☞ There are two ways to place the decoration inside the hangers.
1. Cut the paper with a 1" margin larger than the traced line. Fold the paper down around the edges of the hanger and apply glue.
2. Cut the decorated part out on the traced lines. Hole-punch around the edges of the decorated part. Wrap a piece of tape around a length of yarn that is about four feet long. Tie the untaped end to the hanger. Lace the yarn through the holes. Tie-off the yarn and cut off the excess.

☞ The children can share their hangers and talk about why they drew certain pictures.

☞ The children who have lost a family member might put a garment that belonged to that person on the hanger to remind them of that person's love and their love for that person. If the activity is used in a grief support group and the person is living, the hanger can be a gift.

☞ As the children leave, suggest that they look around them when they want to feel close to the one that died. What did that person leave that reminds them of their loved one's love?

The Garden Angel

By Jan Czech

Illustrated by Susan Aitken

BOOK SUMMARY

Camilla's grandpa died before he could plant his garden. Camilla is reminded of him as she smells his tobacco and lotion. She wears his cap and caresses his cane.

The funeral is on a rainy day. Her grandpa had loved that kind of day. Camilla is very sad, but unable to cry.

Camilla helps her mother clean Grandpa's room. They find his seed catalogs and Camilla asks her mother to allow her to plant the garden. Her mother gives her permission and explains that someone is coming to till the ground. Camilla can then plant the garden.

Camilla remembers what Grandpa taught her and worked hard on the garden. She wears Grandpa's shirt and cap and carries his cane. The cane was used to make the holes to put the seeds in.

Only the head of Grandpa's scarecrow is left. Camilla stuffs the scarecrow with straw, dresses it in Grandpa's clothes and cap, and puts Grandpa's quilt around the shoulders of the scarecrow. The quilt looks like wings. Camilla begins to cry. She feels it is the best garden that Grandpa ever planted.

SUGGESTIONS FOR USE OF THE BOOK

The pictures are large and colorful. They help tell the story. Number the pages, beginning with the first full page of text.

The story can be read in four parts. Select questions you think are appropriate for the ages and needs of the children. If the book is used with one or two children, the questions can be become a plan to guide a more natural conversation. Provide waiting time for children to think and to study the pictures.

Use the picture on page 2 to introduce Camllia. Ask the children to predict why an ambulance might be leaving her home. Share the front of the book and the title. Tell the children that they will find out more about the scarecrow as you read the story.

QUESTIONS FOR GUIDING THE DISCUSSION

Part 1. The death of Grandpa, pages 1-2.
1. How do you think it feels to be hollow inside? Did you feel that way when your family member died?
2. What things reminded Camilla of her grandpa?
3. Why did Grandpa die?
4. Camllia could not cry. How did she feel when she saw her mother crying?

Part 2. The funeral, pages 3-4.
1. Why did Camilla not get under the tent?
2. Why do you think Grandpa liked rainy days?
3. Why did Camilla talk about the red clay?
4. Have you ever heard geese honk? Is it a happy sound?

Part 3. Planning the garden, pages 5-8.
1. Camilla hugged the seed catalogs. What do you think she was thinking?
2. Do think Grandpa's quilt made Camilla feel better?
3. How did Camilla know that the day was not a good one for planting seeds?
4. What do you think of when you think of spring? Was this a good time for the seeds to come?
5. Why did Camilla eat a bowl of raisin cereal?
6. Study the picture on page 10. What do you think Camilla might be thinking?
7. As Camilla planted the seeds, she had tears behind her eyes. What does this mean? Have you felt that way?

Part 4. Preparing the scarecrow, pages 13-16.
1. Were you surprised at what Camllia put on the scarecrow? Why or why not?
2. How did Camilla use the hangers?
3. Grandpa had told Camilla to "make do with what you have"? What did he mean? How did Camilla do this?
4. Do you think Grandpa would have been proud of the garden? Why?
5. Camilla finally cried. Do you think this made her feel better? Did crying make you feel better?

FOLLOW-UP ACTIVITY

☞ Each child can create a collage scarecrow on a large sheet of tan or white construction paper. Have blue paper for the overalls. Have other colors of paper or scraps of cloth available for the shirt and cap. Use raffia ribbon cut into slender pieces or yellow strips of construction paper for the straw. Cut the head from white or yellow paper. Glue pieces of cloth on the scarecrow for the quilt. You can use buttons for the eyes. Display the picture on the front cover of the book for the children to see as they work.

☞ Older children might think of garments worn by their loved one and dress the scarecrow as Camillia did.

☞ You could provide stencils and pre-cut pieces of cloth for the younger children to create the scarecrow's clothing.

☞ The children can draw flowers and vegetable plants.

☞ As the children talk about their scarecrows and Camllia's scarecrow, remind them of why the scarecrow is in the garden. Camllia felt that the scarecrow was a reminder of her grandfather. Ask the children to discuss why this was true.

☞ Why did Camllia think her scarecrow looked like an angel?

☞ Discuss the importance of the rain in the story. The children might want to add some drops to their picture. Rain makes the garden grow. Rain in our life helps us grow. What might the rain represent? Older children might talk about the analogy of rain and tears. Both wash what is around them. Both leave a promise of better things behind them.

The Memory Box

By Kirsten McLaughlin
Illustrated by Adrienne Rudolph

BOOK SUMMARY

A small child's grandfather dies. The child remembers the funeral of his pet rabbit. He is angry at his grandpa because Grandpa had promised to take him fishing. He knew that he would never go fishing or searching for outside creatures with his grandpa again. He would never play ball or go to the ice cream parlor with his grandpa again.

The child's mother helps him understand that it is okay to feel angry. She encourages him to talk about the things that he and his grandpa did. His mother helps him understand that memories are important because they remind us of special times and people.

The child decides to make a memory box. He uses his grandpa's tackle box because it reminds him of fishing trips the two had made. He includes the reading glasses Grandpa wore when he read to the child at night. He includes a packet of seeds to remind him of the garden he and his grandpa had planted. He includes a fishing lure, a picture of himself and Grandpa, and Grandpa's wallet to remind him of trips to the store with Grandpa.

Mother is in the hammock that Grandpa loved. The child takes his memory box to her, and they talk about the memories as they lay in Grandpa's favorite place.

The child continues to plant seeds, and lie in the hammock, and visit the memory box to remind himself of his grandpa. The memory box makes him smile.

SUGGESTIONS FOR USE OF THE BOOK

The author includes a note to caregivers. She hopes that the book will be used as a resource for children who have a family member who is dying or has died. An adult can use the story to share information about death that young children need.

The book is appropriate for classroom teachers who want to help a child cope with death. The child's classmates can then better understand the emotional needs of that child.

You can use this book with an individual child or a small group. When only one or two children are involved, use the questions as the basis for conversation. Facilitators of small groups will want to weave the questions into a conversation with the children. All children should be encouraged to share, but no child should feel pressured to share.

Number pages of the book, beginning with the first full-page picture. The story is divided into five parts for discussion. The pictures help tell the story. Give the children think time as you read and share the pictures. Welcome their comments while sharing the story.

QUESTIONS FOR GUIDING THE DISCUSSION

Part 1. The young child's anger, pages 1-10.
1. Have you ever had a pet that died? Was there a funeral for the pet? How were the funeral of your pet and the funeral of your loved alike? How were the funerals different?
2. What did the young child know about death?
3. What were the things the child did with his grandpa that he would miss?
4. What things did you do with your loved one that you will miss?
5. The young child was angry. He felt his grandpa broke a promise. He felt his grandpa had left him. Did you feel angry when your loved one died? Why?

Part 2. The importance of memories, pages 11-16.
1. Why is it important that we talk about how we feel? What people can you talk to?
2. What is meant when we say that someone has been a "part of our life"? Can that part of your life be taken from you?

Page 3. A memory box, pages 17-30.
1. What things did the child put in his memory box? How did he select these items?
2. What things would you put in a memory box? Why did you suggest these things? What memories do they bring to you?

Part 4. Special memories, pages 21-22.
1. Why was the hammock special to the boy's grandpa? Is there a special place that your loved one had? Do you go and sit there?
2. What memories did the boy and his mother share?

Part 5. Making memories last, pages 23-24.
1. What did the boy do to keep his memories alive?
2. What do you think you might do to keep the memories of your loved one alive?
3. Why does the memory box make the child smile?

FOLLOW-UP ACTIVITY

☞ Children who are old enough to write can make a list of things that they might put in a memory box. Parents can be informed about the creation of the memory box and help the child find the things to put in the box. Small toys or items given to the child by the loved one could be included. The younger children can decorate a box and work with their parents to place memories in the box.

☞ Provide a shoe box or a box from a hobby store for each child. Because the memories of the children are different, they can decorate the boxes in different ways. The children can wrap the boxes and decorate the wrapping with cut out drawings and words to label some of the memories. Cover the top of the box separately. Use index cards to allow the child to draw a memory or two to place in the box. The children can then fill the box at home.

☞ Encourage each child to share a memory to include in the box. Remind the children that the child in the story shared the box with his mother. Encourage the children to talk to family members about the memories. Remind them that it is okay to cry.

☞ The facilitator might share a personal experience that he or she has done to keep a memory alive with a continuous action such as planting a garden. If any of the children have an idea for a project, ask them to share, and encourage them to begin or continue the project. Remind the children that these memories keep the person alive in their hearts.

A Mural for Mamita/ Un Mural Para Mamita

By Alesia K. Alexander
Illustrated by Kyra Teis

BOOK SUMMARY

Luz's grandmother, Mamita, runs the neighborhood store. Luz helps her sweep and dust the store. Pictures of all the family members are on display behind the cash register. One picture shows the grandma in pigtails when she was the age of Luz. Luz wears her hair in the same way. Luz's grandma, Mamita, hugs Luz often. Mamita has a shoe box that contains surprises for Luz. There was often a new surprise in the box.

Mamita becomes ill and was unable to work in the store. Luz's mother explains death to help Luz understand that everything must die someday. Each day Luz paints a picture at school to take home to Mamita.

One day she learns that Mamita has died. She tears up the picture of the sun that she had painted for Mamita that day. The boys and girls at school paint pictures for Luz. That made her feel better. Luz gets an idea from these pictures. She asks others to help her prepare a large mural in Mamita's memory. The entire family begins to plan.

Everyone in the neighborhood comes to paint or watch. Luz paints a large sun as her part of the mural. There is a party for the neighborhood. Luz was given the task of keeping a candle burning near the mural in memory of Mamita.

SUGGESTIONS FOR USE OF THE BOOK

The book shares the story in both Spanish and English. The pictures are large and colorful. Use the pictures and tell or read the story. There are three parts of the story. Read each part and share the pictures. Provide a brief discussion after each part. Select the questions that fit the needs of the children. If there is only one child, use the questions to guide a conversation.

The front and back covers are different. Number the pages, beginning with the first full paged picture.

Use the English front cover to introduce Mamita, Grandma. Ask the children if they have ever helped paint a mural. Have they seen a mural in a building, or on a building? A mural is going to be painted in the story. The things around Mamita's picture will be in the mural.

Show the Spanish front cover to introduce Luz. Explain that her name is the Spanish word for light. What do they think she is painting? Ask them to listen carefully and decide why Luz chose to paint the sun.

Use page 5 to show Luz and her Mamita in the store. What kind of store is it? Let's read and find out about the store and Luz.

Our story really begins with the ending of the story. Let's see what is happening.
(Share the first picture.) Looks like there is a party.

QUESTIONS FOR GUIDING THE DISCUSSION

Part 1. Mamita, Luz, and the store, pages 1-8.
1. How was Mamita special?
2. How could the girl miss a grandfather that she never knew?
3. Do you think Luz's family love each other? Why?
4. How can memories make you strong? Do you have a memory that has made you strong?
5. How do you think Luz got her name? (Candles lit on the day she was born.)
6. Do you think you would enjoy working in a grocery store? What would you do to help?
7. Why do you think Mamita kept the box for Luz?
8. Why do you think Luz loved Mamita so much? Was her love only because of the gifts?

Part 2. The illness and death of Mamita, pages 9-12.
1. When does Luz look into her box of surprises? Why do these things make her feel happy when she is really sad? Do you have something that belonged to your loved one that makes you feel happier? What is the item? Why does it make you feel better?
2. How did Luz's family help while her Mamita had cancer? Did you help in some way when your family member was ill? (Remember that not all deaths come after an illness. This question may not always be appropriate.)

3. What did Luz's mother tell her about death? (Show the picture of Luz and the torn picture.) What is at Luz's feet?
4. Did Luz's teacher help her when Mamita was ill and when Mamita died? How? Did you have someone at school who helped you?

Part 3. A mural for Mamita, pages 13-18.
1. How were plans for the mural made?
2. What did Pedro draw? (Revisit the front cover.) Why do you think these pictures were chosen?
3. Did you find out why Luz painted the sun? What colors did she use? Why do you think she used these colors?
4. You now know about the party. Let's look again at the first picture. What is happening in the picture?
5. Do you think the people at the party felt good about their mural in honor of Mamita?
6. How does Luz feel?

FOLLOW-UP ACTIVITY

☞ Children can make a sun plaque to hang on the wall in memory of the loved one can be made.

☞ Use a red or yellow paper plate or a yellow cutout circle for the sun.

☞ Provide red, yellow and orange construction paper for children to cut triangles, rectangles, and circles to decorate the plaque. A ring of triangles can be glued, or stapled, to the plate or circle. Between each triangle, glue a small rectangle of another color. Glue small circles on the inner circle of the plate or circle.

☞ Add eyes, a nose, a mouth, and cheeks with black cutouts.

☞ Use a strip of red, orange, or yellow paper to form a loop to be used to display the plaque. Glue this loop to the back of the plaque.

☞ As the children share their plaques, talk about the warmth of the sun. Discuss how the sun can make them warm when they are cold. Elicit responses that share why the sun was a good thing for Luz to paint. Ask if the children think Luz's sun made her feel warm and why.

☞ Encourage the children to take the plaque home and hang near a picture of their loved one. They might light a candle, with the help of an adult, by the plaque and picture. How does each bring warmth?

Babka's Serenade

By Marianne Zebrowski
Illustrated by Kyra Teis

BOOK SUMMARY

A young girl named Gail and her grandmother, Babka, have great fun in the grandma's garden. They talk about pretend fairies. Babka tells Gail stories that make her feel like a princess. Babka dies and Gail does not want to eat. She attends the funeral, but has trouble believing that she will never see Babka again.

After the funeral, Gail sits in the grandma's garden, but the magic is gone. The garden bench and other things that belonged to Babka are put in the garage. She cries for the first time.

Springtime comes. The girl and her mother decide to plant a garden in memory of Babka. When the flowers bloom, the bench is brought out to the new garden. Gail sits in the new garden. The magic is back. She hears music. She can hear her grandma inviting her to come hear more stories.

SUGGESTIONS FOR USE OF THE BOOK

Elementary age children will find the colorful pictures a support to the story. Number the pages, beginning with the first full-page picture.

For discussion, divide the story into three parts. Select questions that fit the ages and interests of children in the group.

Use the front cover to introduce the girl. She is sitting in the garden where she and Babka played and talked. Use the picture on page 6 to introduce Babka and mother. Explain that Babka is the mother of the girl's mother.

Ask the children if they know what a "serenade" is. After the group understands the word, tell them to listen carefully to find when the music was heard and why it was heard. Is it heard a second time?

QUESTIONS FOR GUIDING THE DISCUSSION

Part 1. Babka and the garden, pages 1-6.
1. Why did the girl enjoy the garden?
2. What kind of things did she and Babka imagine?
3. Do you ever play a game that lets you imagine things? What do you imagine? Who is with you when you do this?
4. Why did the young child want to be like the girl in her grandma's story?
5. Why did the young child's mama shake her head?

Part 2. The death and funeral of Babka, pages 7-12.
1. What did the author mean when she said that the young child had a "hole in her stomach"?
2. Why do you suppose she kicked the legs of her chair during the funeral?
3. When did the girl cry?

Part 3. Happenings after Babka's death, rest of book.
1. What was the girl angry about? What did she wonder? Could she have prevented the death?
2. Why did the girl decide that she wanted a garden?
3. Do you think her mother liked the idea of making a garden? Why do you think her mother's face became red?
4. Did the girl have to ask her parents to bring the bench into the garden? Why not?
5. What did the girl mean when she called the garden a "magic place"?
6. What "magic" thing makes you think of your loved one?
7. Does the girl hear music again? What is the music?
8. How did the girl show her love for Babka?

FOLLOW-UP ACTIVITY

☞ Ask the children to discuss the role of flowers in the story. You might talk about why flowers are part of a funeral.

☞ The children can create a beautiful picture of flowers on a sheet of white construction paper.

☞ Prepare tempera paint in small containers. You will need green and at least two colors for the flowers.

☞ Provide old shirts for children to wear as they use the paint.

☞ Cut toilet tissue tubes into about four pieces. Pinch each small ring to make a petal shape.

☞ Have uncut tubes available for the children to use as a round shape.

☞ The children can do scattered flowers on the paper, or they can paint stems for the flowers that might be in a bunch or a vase. The completed picture can be stapled to a sheet of colored construction paper.

☞ The children dip the cardboard sections into the paint to print flowers and leaves on the paper. Remind the children to use each cardboard section in only one color.

☞ Close the session by talking about the paintings. The children may want to discuss the flowers seen at the funerals of their loved ones. They can revisit the pictures from "Babka's Serenade". You could play quiet music as the children discuss the pictures.

☞ Suggest that the children take their flower art home and place it beside a picture of their loved one.

Lilacs for Grandma

By Margaret Whitler Hucek
Illustrated by Kristi McClendon

BOOK SUMMARY

A large lilac bush grows outside Grandma's house. This is Megan's favorite hiding place. She hides there as the story begins. Her grandma is ill, and Megan wants to know what is happening. Her mother has told her to stay out of the way.

Megan sees her aunts arrive and hears her grandma say that she is going to the hospital. Megan wanted to visit the hospital, but her mother does not let her.

Grandma comes home from the hospital. Miss Angela comes to help care for Grandma. Megan wonders why her mother and her aunts are crying.

Grandma sends for Megan. She tells Megan that she is dying and asks the girl to bring her a bouquet of lilacs each morning and to come each evening to open her window so she can watch the dove's nest and the dove family.

Grandma dies. On the day of the funeral, Megan takes a bouquet of lilacs to her Grandma's grave. She and her mother decide to plant some small lilac bushes around the pond.

SUGGESTIONS FOR USE OF THE BOOK

The story can be separated into five parts. Read each part and select appropriate questions to elicit comments and feelings from the children. If you are working with one or two children, reword the questions to become part of the conversation following each section of the book.

QUESTIONS FOR GUIDING THE DISCUSSION

Part 1. Grandma's house, pages 2-7.
1. What did we find out about Megan's family?
2. Do you have a favorite place that you go to when you want to be alone? Where is it? What do you do?

3. What clues help us know that Grandma loved Megan and her brother?
4. What memories do you have of a grandparent's home?
5. When did Megan usually come out of her hiding place?
6. Why is today different?

Part 2. Grandma is ill, pages 8-11.
1. What do you think a "work-up" at the hospital is?
2. What did Grandma ask Megan to do for her?
3. Why do you think Grandma was in the hospital so long?
4. How was Grandma different after she came home from the hospital?
5. What happened to the dove's nest?

Part 3. Megan's conversation with Grandma, pages 12-17.
1. Why did Megan cry when she told her Grandma about the dove's nest? Did Grandma seem to be worried about the nest? Why?
2. What had Grandma promised Megan she could do when spring came?
3. What did Grandma tell Megan?
4. How did the memories of the "lilac seasons" help Grandma?
5. Grandma knew she would become so ill that she could not talk to Megan. Why did she want Megan to continue to come and see her?

Part 4. Grandma's death, pages 18-19.
1. What did Megan want to do when her grandma died?
2. Why do you think Megan filled Grandma's vase with lilacs again?
3. Did the dove and her family return? Why do you think Megan said she thought that Grandma would have liked the dove family?

Part 5. The day of the funeral, pages 20-21.
1. What did Megan do on the day of the funeral?
2. Why did she wait until everyone was gone to put the lilacs on the grave?
3. What did her mother suggest that Megan should do?

FOLLOW-UP ACTIVITY

☞ The children can create a dove from a piece of heavy gray or white paper and folded pieces of paper.

☞ Draw the shape of a bird's body on stiff paper. Cut out the body.

☞ Cut two slits in the body. One slit will be for the wings of the bird. The other slit will be for the bird's tail.

☞ Cut a piece of white paper in half. Fold each piece like an accordion, length-wise. If you desire you can cut small notches into the edges of the folded pieces of paper.

☞ Insert one piece of folded paper into the slit for the wings. Insert the other into the slit for the tail. Secure both to the body with scotch tape.

☞ Draw an eye on each side of the bird.

☞ Tape some string to the body of the bird, so it can be hung.

☞ Discuss the role the dove family played in the story. You can share the following facts about doves with the children:

• The mother dove is a careless builder. She builds a flimsy nest that is usually made of a few sticks that are placed loosely together. Could this explain why the nest fell so easily?

• The birds make cooing sounds. Grandma enjoyed these sounds. Why do you think she enjoyed the sounds?

• Doves feed on grass seeds and grain. What did Megan feed the doves in the story? Why did she care enough to feed the birds?

• Most adult doves are about one foot long. (Study the picture on page 5.) The baby birds grow quickly. That is one reason it is so much fun to watch the bird family.

• The dove is said to be the bird of "peace." What is peace? How did the doves help Megan find peace?

The Christmas Cactus

By Elizabeth Wrenn

Illustrated by Susan Aitken

BOOK SUMMARY

It is the Christmas season, and Megan's grandmother, Nana, is in the hospital. Megan is caring for Nana's plants and feeling very angry. She tosses her grandmother's gardening hat and notices a small plant that needs to be watered.

The phone rings. It is Megan's mother telling Megan and her father to come to the hospital. Megan takes the small plant with her. Her father suggests that they need to tell Nana that they love her.

Megan feels very sad when she sees her sick grandmother. Nana tells her that it is okay to cry. Megan shows Nana the plant. Nana tells Megan that dying is like the life of the Christmas cactus. During the year, the plant grows. When Christmas comes, a tiny bud opens and something beautiful happens. At the end of life we bloom and become something new and beautiful. She tells Megan to water the plant and give it light, but not the direct rays of the sun. When the plant blooms, Megan is to think of her.

Megan cares for the cactus. Her family tries to celebrate Christmas. On Christmas day Megan sees a spot of red on the cactus. She then sees the beautiful flower that reminds her of Nana. She considers the bloom to be a gift from Nana.

SUGGESTION FOR USE OF THE BOOK

This is a great book to use in a grief support program during the Christmas season. Share the book in four sections. Follow each section with a discussion. Number the pages, beginning with the first page of print.

Introduce the book with a real Christmas cactus. Use the front cover to set the background. " What time of year is it? How do you know?"

Use page 2 to introduce Megan. Explain that she is in the sunroom where Nana has her plants. "How do you think Megan feels? Let's listen and find out what is worrying Megan."

QUESTIONS FOR GUIDING THE DISCUSSION

Part 1. Introduction, pages 1-4.
1. Did we find out why Megan is sad?
2. Why does Megan like to be in the sunroom?
3. What things in the sunroom reminded Megan of her Nana?
4. Why do you think Megan feels so angry? Have you felt that way?
5. Why do you think Megan noticed the small plant?

Part 2. Megan visits Nana at the hospital, pages 5-14.
1. What did Megan's father tell her about death?
2. Was Megan wise when she chose the small plant to take to Nana? Why?
3. How can everything be the same and still be different? Do you understand how Megan felt?
4. Why are the reindeer pictures at the bottom of page ten? Do you have a special Christmas memory of your loved one?
5. What did Nana call Megan? Why do you think she called her that? Do you have a nickname that your loved one used for you? What was it? Is there a story behind the name?
6. Why did Megan's parents leave the hospital room?
7. What words do you think can describe how Megan felt as she visited with Nana?
8. What did Nana tell Megan about death?
9. What did Nana tell Megan to do?

Part 3. Christmas without Nana, pages 15-18.
1. Why is the picture on page 16 in black and white?
2. What emotion is missing in the picture and in Megan's life?
3. Why was Megan finally able to cry? When did you cry?
4. Why was Nana's hat in Megan's room and not in the sunroom?

Part 4. A special gift from Nana, pages 19-22.
1. Why did Megan not go to the Christmas tree when she first got up?
2. What did the author mean when she said that the snow could not fill the "hole inside" Megan?
3. Was Megan able to cry again?
4. Why did Megan's heart start thumping?
5. Do you think Megan really received a present from her grandmother? Explain.

FOLLOW-UP ACTIVITY

☞ If the timing is correct, show a Christmas cactus to the child/children. The children can make a collage plant to help them remember the story and its meaning.

☞ You will need green and pink paper for the plant, brown paper for the pot and a sheet of construction or manila paper for the background. You could provide a stencil to trace the pot on the brown paper.

☞ Glue the pot on the background paper. The pot should cover between one third to one half of the sheet.

☞ After the children have studied the green segments of the cactus plant have them cut small pieces of green to use in forming the plant. If you are working within a short time-frame, you may want to cut these pieces ahead of time.

☞ Have the children cut some pink blossoms and tiny buds from the pink paper. Use the front cover and last page of the book to help the children see the blossoms.

☞ Draw a line of glue where a branch of the plant will be. Attach the small green pieces to the glue. Repeat this process for two or three more branches. Using the glue to draw the line will save time.

☞ Glue the blossoms onto the plant.

☞ As the session closes, review the analogy of dying and the Christmas cactus. You might explain that the flower will soon fall from the cactus, but the cactus will continue to live. Explain how that is what happened to their loved one. They can't be seen, but they continue to live in our hearts and memories.

Grandfather Hurant Lives Forever

By Susanna Pitzer

Illustrated by Kyra Teis

BOOK SUMMARY

Grigor's grandfather works in a rug shop. He repairs and sells rugs. When Grigor visits the shop, his grandfather gives him cinnamon candy and helps Grigor make a rug. Grigor is very proud of his grandfather and what he does.

Grandfather tells Grigor about the country of Armenia and how he came to America. He told how he saved his money to make the rug shop a reality. Grandfather helps Grigor weave his first rug. They attach this to the rug: "Grigor and Hurant Gedigan, Rug Makers". Grigor begins to work on his second rug.

Grandfather becomes ill and goes to the hospital. The boy goes to the hospital to visit his grandfather. Grandfather tells Grigor that he will always be with him. Grigor tells his grandfather that they can make rugs together.

Grandfather dies. Grigor feels sorry for his mother, but becomes very angry. He remembers his grandfather's promise. Grigor feels sad, but cannot cry at the funeral. For over a week he throws things and is angry all of the time. One day he takes the rug that his grandfather helped him make and wraps it around himself. The rug makes him feel better.

Grigor goes back to the rug shop. He sits in his grandfather's chair and eats some cinnamon candy. He begins to work on the second rug. As he works on the rug, Grigor can see his grandfather. The new rug will have a label that says, "Grandfather Hurant Lives Forever."

SUGGESTION FOR USE OF THE BOOK

The story has five parts. Read the story in parts and use questions that fit the needs and ages of the children. The colors used in the illustrations help set the mood for each part of the story. The use of shilouette in black emphasizes the sad parts of the story. Number the pages, beginning with the first page of text.

The front and back covers show a rug made by Grigor. Share that picture and the title of the book. Use page 4 to introduce the boy and his grandfather. Explain that the pictures used in the rug tell the story of the grandfather and the country that he grew up in, Armenia. Ask the children to listen to learn how Grandfather Hurant lives forever.

QUESTIONS FOR GUIDING THE DISCUSSION

Part 1. Grandfather's rug shop, pages 1-4.
1. Why do you think Grigor told his grandfather that he wasn't little anymore?
2. What did the words say on the rug grandfather was mending?
3. Why did Grigor think his grandfather was talented? Was there a talent, or special ability, that your loved one who died had? Do you have a special talent?

Part 2. Grigor becomes a rug maker, pages 5-8.
1. What memories came to Grandfather as he signed his rugs in Armenian? Share the picture on page 6. Who are the people in the picture?
2. What label was put on Grigor's first rug? How do you think this made Grigor feel?
3. What did Grigor tell his grandfather that he wanted to be when he grew up? Why do you think Grigor felt this way?
4. What do you think you want to do when you grow up? Why?
5. Why did Grigor's cheeks hurt? How was he feeling?

Part 3. Grandfather goes to the hospital, pages 9-12.
1. Show picture on page 11. Why do you think the illustrator used black in the picture?
2. How could Mother hold Grigor too tightly? Why did she do this?
3. Have you ever visited anyone in the hospital? Who? How did you feel?
4. What do you remember seeing in the hospital room that you visited?
5. What did Grandfather promise Grigor in a soft voice?

Part 4. Grandfather dies, pages 13-16.
1. How did Grigor feel when he heard that his grandfather had died? How did you feel when you heard that your loved one had died? Explain that feeling.
2. Why was Grigor so angry at his grandfather? How did he show his anger?
3. Show the picture on page 16. What has Grigor done?
4. Do you think Grigor was being honest with himself when he said he did not want to be a rugmaker?
5. Are you angry at your family member who died? If you are over your anger, how did you find comfort?

Part 5. Grigor returns to the rug shop, pages 17-20.
1. Did Grigor go into the rug shop the first time he went back to it? Why?
2. Did Grigor have to be brave to go inside the shop? Why was his heart beating fast?
3. Why did Mr. Kashian suggest that Grigor sit in his grandfather's chair? What did he tell Grigor about his grandfather?
4. What things reminded Grigor of his grandfather?
5. Why did Grigor decide that his grandfather had not lied to him?
6. What Armenian words did Grigor put on his second rug?
7. How could Grigor's grandfather live forever?
8. How can your loved one live forever?

FOLLOW-UP ACTIVITY

☞ The children can cut black shilouettes, glue them on yellow construction paper, and illustrate the background. Ask the children to think of something that they did with their loved one. They will sketch that memory as the black part of the picture.

☞ Ideas for the picture can come from pages 2 and 9. Each child will need black construction paper, a sheet of yellow construction paper, scissors, glue and crayons or colored markers.

☞ The children can draw the large shilouette part of the picture with white crayon, then cut out the silhouette and glue it onto the yellow sheet.

☞ Have the children use bright colors to complete the picture.

☞ Encourage the children to talk about their pictures as they work. Why did they select the ideas they used? What memories do they have?

☞ Before the children leave, remind them of the name of the book. Ask why the author chose that title. Talk about how Grigor's grandfather still lives and how their family member still lives.

☞ Encourage the children to share their picture with their family. They might practice sharing the ideas that they can share with the family.

SECTION 4
USING STORYBOOKS TO EXPLAIN GRIEF AND LOSS AFTER THE DEATH OF A SIBLING

Lost and Found, Remembering a Sister

By Ellen Yeomans
Illustrated by Dee deRosa

BOOK SUMMARY

The storyteller's sister, Paige, dies from cancer. The grandparents say the family had lost Paige. The parents say Paige died. The surviving sister does not say anything. Family and friends come to the house. Everyone looks scared and tries not to cry. The sister wonders if she could find Paige.

After the funeral the dad is mad, and Mother cries all of the time. The young sister feels she is in the way. She loses interest in dancing lessons. The family sells their van. Nighttime is hard for her. She doesn't have her big sister to sleep with and to help her feel safe.

When school starts the little sister does not know where to sit on the bus without her sister. Her teacher buys her a new dress for school. Mom does not feel like shopping. The young child's classmates talk about their families. When the young child tries to draw Paige's picture, she cries in front of everyone.

The young child finds comfort in her sister's blanket. At school she draws a picture of light. She takes the picture home to her parents, and the picture helps them. Mom stops crying all the time, and Dad is not mad all of the time. The young child can talk about her sister.

The teacher keeps Paige's sweater where the sister can touch it. The school plants a tree in Paige's memory. Paige's books and favorite toys bring comfort to her sister. Paige is not lost forever. She is in the hearts of those who loved her.

SUGGESTION FOR USE OF THE BOOK

You can read the story in five parts, with a discussion after each part. You will want to be familiar with the symbols of light and the butterfly. The butterfly is not a part of the story, but is in several of the illustrations. It is also on the front cover of the book.

Ask the children to share words and phrases used to discuss the death of a person. Share the front cover and title. Talk about the meaning of the word "lost". Is this really what happens when someone dies? Ask the children to listen and discover what the storyteller discovers about death.

QUESTIONS FOR GUIDING THE DISCUSSION

Part 1. The death of a big sister, pages 1-4.
1. Why do you suppose Grandma said that Paige was lost?
2. Show the picture on page 2. What does the empty chair represent?
3. Who was right about what had happened to Paige?
4. Why did the family, friends, family members, doctors and nurses come to see the young sister and her parents?
5. Show the pictures on pages 3 and 4. Why do the people look like black shadows?

Part 2. After the funeral, pages 5-10.
1. Show the picture on pages 5 and 6. What does the picture represent? Why do you think the artist used this picture? How did the girl and her parents feel?
2. Why did the younger sister not want to go to dance lessons? Is there some place that you do not like to go without your loved one who died? Is there something you do not want to do without your loved one?
3. Why do you think the parents sold the van?
4. What was the most difficult part of the day for the young sister? Are nights difficult for you? If so, why?
5. Why did the girl need a nightlight and want to leave her door open?

Part 3. Back to school, pages 12-18.
1. Why did the girl not know where to sit on the bus?
2. Why did the teacher buy the girl a new dress? Do you think the teacher cares about the girl?
3. Why did the girl cry at school? Have you had an experience at school that made you sad, or made you cry? Can you share that experience?
4. Show the picture on page 15. Why is the picture of Paige smaller than that of the sister? We were told that Paige was the big sister. Why is that part of the picture smudged looking?
5. Show the picture on page 16. What does this picture represent? Was it really raining?

Part 4. Things begin to change, pages 17-22.
1. What do you think the light represents?
2. What helped the girl begin to feel the light and warmth of comfort? What did she realize about her sister?
3. Show the picture on pages 19 and 20. What do the hearts represent? The star? The cloud of light?
4. Show the hands on pages 21 and 22. Are these big or little hands? What are the hands doing? Whose hands are they?

Part 5. Special sources of comfort, pages 23-32.
1. Do you think the teacher knew Paige? Why would she leave the coat hanging in a closet?
2. What did the children think about when they saw or decorated the tree?
3. Why is there a butterfly in the picture? What is the butterfly doing? Is the little sister beginning to fly again?
4. What special things remind you of your loved one who died?
5. Study the picture of the butterflies on the last two pages. Is the girl feeling free like the flying butterflies? Why?

FOLLOW-UP ACTIVITY

- The children can make a butterfly from two small, lightweight paper plates. Each child will need scissors, two paper plates, and crayons or colored pens. You will need a stapler.

- Draw the butterfly's body in the exact center of one plate. Draw the wings of the butterfly. Make the butterfly the size of the plate. Color the butterfly.

- Fold the butterfly in half with the colored wings facing each other.

- Cut the second paper plate in half. Trim one inch off the straight edge of each half.

- Staple the cut plate to the back of the plate with the butterfly picture on it.

- The child can insert his hand in the back parts of the butterfly and make the wings move.

- At one point in the story, the young child felt fenced in and like a prisoner. Talk with the children about how the young child in the story began to feel free and see some light in her life. How did this happen? Ask the children if they are still feeling fenced in, or are they beginning to see some light? Remind them that someday, they too can feel like flying again.

Since My Bother Died/ Desde Que Murió Mi Hermano

By Marisol Muñoz-Kiehne

Illustrated by Glenda Dietrich

BOOK SUMMARY

The story is told in first person by a young child whose brother has died. At first he has trouble believing that the brother had died. People do not know what to say to him. He wants it all to be a dream.

The young child becomes very angry. He wonders if he could have prevented his brother's death. He is sorry that he had become angry with his brother.

He wonders if his parents wish that he had died instead of his brother. He is finally able to cry. Sometimes his mind goes blank and he doesn't care about anything. He has headaches and stomachaches. He wants to be a baby again.

The young child is often scared. He worries about forgetting his brother. He shares memories of ball games, music and dancing.

Painting helps the young child. Sometimes his paintings are messy; sometimes they are neat. The brother is alive in his heart. He plans to continue to paint memories of the brother.

SUGGESTION FOR USE OF THE BOOK

The book has both English and Spanish texts. The author provides two introductions, "A Note to Parents and Caregivers" and "A Note to Teachers and Caregivers". These pages contain ideas for providing support for the child who has lost a family member to death. They include good hints for conversation with the child and suggest special activities to help the child cope with the death.

The artwork in the book consists of shilouette pictures and hints of a rainbow. The first pictures are of drab colors. As the story develops, the pictures become more colorful, until there is finally a rainbow. Younger children may not understand the hidden meanings of the pictures, but the intermediate level elementary children will probably enjoy the message of the pictures.

Number the pages, beginning with the first page of the text. The story has three parts. Read the book one section at a time and select questions for use with a group. If you are working with one or two children, use the questions to guide your conversation after each part of the book.

QUESTIONS TO GUIDE THE DISCUSSION

Part 1. The storyteller's anger, pages 1-4.
1. In what ways has the storyteller's life changed?
2. How was the storyteller's life like a nightmare?
3. The storyteller has a lot of questions. What are some questions that you asked after the death of your family member?
4. Why does he feel guilty? Is he guilty? Have you felt that way?

Part 2. The storyteller's feelings and emotions, pages 5-8.
1. What are emotions that the storyteller experiences? Why does he feel so different at different times? Has this happened to you? Explain.
2. What does the storyteller mean by "point of living"? What are the reasons for wanting to live?
3. Why do you think the boy wants to be by himself?
4. Do you worry about forgetting your family member who died? What can you do about that worry?

Part 3. How the storyteller finds comfort, pages 9-12.
1. If you were to paint pictures of your loved one, what would that person be doing?
2. What could the yellow bits at the bottom of page ten represent?
3. Compare a page from the first part of the book and this page. Why are the colors on this page brighter?

FOLLOW-UP ACTIVITY

☞ If you are working with a group of children who have lost a family member, the children will be at different points in their journey of coping. Some of the children may identify with the drab colored pages and the sad thing. Others may relate to the bright colors.

☞ Provide heavy white paper, water color paints, brushes, and colored pens or crayons.

☞ Have each child sketch a shilouette picture and color it with crayons or pens.

☞ The rainbow trail will be done with the watercolors, the crayons, or the colored pens. The picture can be a sad or a happy memory.

☞ As the children work, encourage them to share the memories and why they were chosen. If some of the children use the brighter, happier colors, suggest that they share how they have been able to cope with their emotions.

☞ After listening to the children's memories, share some information about rainbows.

- Rainbows are seen only after a rain. The rain can represent the sad things. The rainbow is the promise of better things to come.

- Hundreds of tiny droplets bend the rays of light to cause the rainbow. Tears can help bring the rainbow and make us feel better.

- Rainbows are really round. We only see half of the rainbow. There are happier times that we cannot see yet.

- Keeping the one that died in our hearts can help us see the rainbow and its promise of better times.

NOTES SECTION

BIOGRAPHIES

Dr. Geraldine Haggard

is a facilitator in *Journey of Hope*, a grief support program in the Dallas area. She works with kindergarten, first, and second graders that have experienced a death in their families. She is on the program committee for the program and writes curriculum based on the use of children's books about grief and related topics. Before her retirement, she had 48 years of experience as a teacher and a trainer of teachers'. Both of her daughters are elementary teachers. She works with pre-schoolers and third graders in her church. As chairman of a committee for her Retired Teachers Association that gives books to low-income students, she writes grants and directs the gifting of over 2,000 books in her hometown annually. Tutoring and volunteer work in her daughter's first grade are weekly activities.

Knoll Graham Gilbert

is a graphic designer from Cincinnati, Ohio, who has been creating book covers and interiors since 2001. With the birth of his first child, Darian Joseph, he needed more money for diapers, so he began doing freelance book design for supplemental income. Since then he has created over thirty titles for various publishers across the United States. He has worked in practically every genre in the field, from science fiction/fantasy to children's literature. As of 4/20/05 he is a proud father of his first baby girl, Eva Kazia. Hence, he is in need of more diaper money, so if you enjoyed his cover and layout design in this fine publication then you may want to check out more of his work at www.portfolio.com/knollgilbert.